WAR ON TERROR
TECHNOLOGY

BY NEL YOMTOV

CONTENT CONSULTANT
Peter Forster, PhD
Senior Lecturer of Information Sciences and Technology
The Pennsylvania State University

Cover image: A Cougar mine-resistant vehicle drives
across a dirt road in Iraq in 2008.

Core Library

An Imprint of Abdo Publishing
abdopublishing.com

abdopublishing.com

Published by Abdo Publishing, a division of ABDO, PO Box 398166,
Minneapolis, Minnesota 55439. Copyright © 2018 by Abdo Consulting
Group, Inc. International copyrights reserved in all countries. No part of this
book may be reproduced in any form without written permission from the
publisher. Core Library™ is a trademark and logo of Abdo Publishing.

Printed in the United States of America, North Mankato, Minnesota
042017
092017

Cover Photo: US Air Force
Interior Photos: US Air Force, 1, 18–19, 21; US Army, 4–5, 10–11, 12–13, 24; DigitalGlobe/Getty
Images, 7; Spencer Platt/Getty Images, 8; US Marine Corps, 16, 45; Chip Somodevilla/Getty
Images, 26–27; Sipa/AP Images, 29; Scott Nelson/Getty Images, 31; Ted S. Warren/AP Images,
34–35; Mohd Rasfan/AFP/Getty Images, 37; Red Line Editorial, 38; Ron Edmonds/AP Images, 39

Editor: Arnold Ringstad
Imprint Designer: Maggie Villaume
Series Design Direction: Nikki Farinella

Publisher's Cataloging-in-Publication Data

Names: Yomtov, Nel, author.
Title: War on terror technology / by Nel Yomtov.
Description: Minneapolis, MN : Abdo Publishing, 2018. | Series: War technology |
    Includes bibliographical references and index.
Identifiers: LCCN 2017930446 | ISBN 9781532111914 (lib. bdg.) |
    ISBN 9781680789768 (ebook)
Subjects: LCSH: War on terrorism, 2001-2009--Technology--Juvenile literature. |
    Technological innovations--History--21st century--Juvenile literature. |
    Terrorism--United States--Prevention--Juvenile literature.
Classification: DDC 356--dc23
    LC record available at http://lccn.loc.gov/2017930446

CONTENTS

FIGHTING A NEW WAR

Early on May 2, 2011, two helicopters flew into Pakistan. They carried US Navy SEALs. The soldiers were going to Abbottabad. The US government believed Osama bin Laden was hiding there. Bin Laden had planned the terrorist attacks of September 11, 2001, which had killed nearly 3,000 Americans. The US government had finally tracked him down.

The helicopters landed. The soldiers ran out and moved into the building. They exchanged gunfire with bin Laden's guards. Then the SEALs moved to the upper floors.

The soldiers on the bin Laden raid flew in specially modified UH-60 Blackhawk helicopters.

Bin Laden peered through his bedroom door. He saw the Americans. The SEALs fired their HK416 rifles. Bin Laden was killed instantly. His body was flown out of Pakistan. US forces buried his body at sea.

The United States used high-tech equipment to find bin Laden. Drones watched the compound from high above. Devices targeted the terrorist group's computers. And stealth helicopters were used on the mission that killed him.

WHAT IS TERRORISM?

The goal of terrorism is to cause fear by spreading panic. Terrorists use this fear to create political

THE SEPTEMBER 11 ATTACKS

On September 11, 2001, 19 terrorists hijacked four US airliners. They flew two of them into the World Trade Center towers in New York City. A third flew into the Pentagon in Washington, DC. This is the headquarters of the US Department of Defense. A fourth plane crashed into a field in Pennsylvania. The passengers on this plane had heard about the other hijackings. They fought back against the terrorists.

Satellite image technology played a part in finding and monitoring bin Laden's compound.

change. Some terrorists want to bring attention to their cause. Others carry out attacks to influence government decisions.

The September 11 attacks were the deadliest terror attacks in US history. Terrorists hijacked airliners. They flew the planes into buildings. Bin Laden's Islamic extremist group, al-Qaeda, was responsible. The attack triggered the War on Terror.

The United States launched the War on Terror in response to the September 11 attacks.

A NEW KIND OF WAR

The War on Terror got its name from President George W. Bush. He was president during the September 11 attacks. This war differed from past US wars. Previous wars were fought against nations. US troops faced organized armies. Wars ended when one side surrendered. But terrorist groups are not governments. They do not wear uniforms. They attack civilians without warning. There is no single leader who can surrender to end the war. The United States had to find new ways to root out terrorist groups.

PERSPECTIVES
FIGHTING TERRORIST GROUPS ONLINE

Terrorist organizations use the Internet to find new members, raise money, and plan attacks. In December 2015, President Barack Obama asked technology companies and police to work together against this. "I will urge high-tech and law-enforcement leaders to make it harder for terrorist leaders to use technology to escape from justice," the president said.

Technology plays an important role in this war. Tough vehicles defend against bombs. Robots keep human soldiers safe. And cyberwarfare tools track terrorist communications. As the War on Terror continues, other new technologies will emerge. Some will be used on foreign battlefields. Others will be used within the United States.

HIGH-TECH WEAPONS

In the fall of 2001, US troops entered Afghanistan. They searched for those who planned the September 11 attacks. They also defeated the nation's government, called the Taliban. The Taliban had supported al-Qaeda.

The United States invaded Iraq in 2003. The government stated that Iraq's leader, Saddam Hussein, was sheltering terrorists. It also said he was building deadly weapons. Most US troops left Iraq by 2011 and Afghanistan by 2014. But by 2017, smaller numbers of soldiers still remained.

US and British troops patrol an area in Afghanistan in 2007.

US troops carrying M4A1 rifles search a house in Afghanistan.

Much of the fighting in these areas was traditional warfare. The two sides fought each other directly. Their weapons included rifles and machine guns. One key US

rifle is the M4A1. It is a favorite of US special-operations troops. The M4A1 can shoot in automatic mode. This means it fires repeatedly if the trigger is held down.

The MK 46 light machine gun and the MK 12 rifle are also used. Both have seen action with the army and navy. The Javelin missile launcher is another key weapon. It was designed to destroy tanks. Troops in the War on Terror have also used it against enemy buildings and caves.

Soldiers carry other equipment too. US soldiers have helmets, gloves, and combat boots. Body armor protects them. Armored plates shield against bullets and explosions. Night-vision goggles allow soldiers to see in dim light. Many troops also carry small

PERSPECTIVES

BATTLEFIELD FEEDBACK

Soldiers tested the XM-25 grenade launcher in Afghanistan. This weapon fires grenades that explode in midair. Feedback from soldiers helped designers make changes to the XM-25. Many said the 14-pound (6.3-kg) weapon was too heavy. XM-25 program manager Colonel Scott Armstrong said, "The Army has learned many valuable lessons. . . . We have already incorporated more than 100 improvements to the systems."

GPS devices. These pieces of equipment let them figure out their exact location.

VEHICLES

One of the biggest threats to US soldiers has been improvised explosive devices (IEDs). These are bombs planted by terrorists. They may be placed along the roadside. The bombs explode when vehicles pass. They damage tanks and trucks. They can also kill the people inside.

Engineers created new vehicles to counter the IED threat. Mine-Resistant Ambush Protected (MRAP) vehicles have saved many lives. These four-wheeled

MISSILE DEFENSE

One threat to military aircraft is a missile fired from the ground. Such missiles locate their target with a guidance system. Many aircraft have equipment to spot and defend against missiles. One example is the Guardian Anti-Missile System. The Guardian detects the energy of the incoming missile. It then disables the guidance system.

vehicles are heavily armored. Their V-shaped structures deflect the force of a blast. An explosion's energy travels around the passenger compartment, rather than straight up through the floor. A soldier is five times less likely to be killed or injured in an MRAP than in a normal vehicle.

EXPLORE ONLINE

IEDs have been deadly threats to US troops in the War on Terror. Read the article about IEDs on the website below. How does this information compare to what is in the text? How is it different?

HOW IEDs WORK

abdocorelibrary.com/war-on-terror-tech

Large numbers of MRAPs were used in Afghanistan and Iraq.

DRONES
AND ROBOTS

Robots became important tools in the War on Terror. Some can fly. Aircraft called drones are flown remotely. Some drones simply watch over an area from above. Others can fire missiles. Drones can be controlled from US bases. Robots are used on the ground, too. They can disable IEDs or search through rubble for survivors.

DRONES

The US military has flown thousands of drone missions in the War on Terror. They target terrorists in the Middle East and Africa. Drones have killed more than 500 suspected terrorist

A drone operator controls an aircraft from a distant location.

leaders. In 2015, a drone strike in Somalia killed a terrorist leader. He had helped plan a 2013 attack in Kenya. A gunman there had killed 67 people.

The MQ-1 Predator is one of the most widely used drones. The Predator can carry two Hellfire missiles. It has seen action in Afghanistan, Iraq, and Yemen. Predators have flown alongside piloted aircraft. They can provide support for troops on the ground. The MQ-9 Reaper is larger. It can fly higher and farther. The Reaper uses missiles and laser-guided bombs.

HACKING DRONES

In 2009, many Predator drones flew over Iraq. They sent video images of their targets to operators in the United States. During one mission, enemy soldiers hacked into a Predator's video feed. This allowed them to see what the Predator was seeing. When their houses came into view, they moved elsewhere. They escaped a possible missile attack. In the future, people could use hacking to steal drones or even turn them against their owners.

THE MQ-1
PREDATOR

This image shows the parts of the Predator drone. Below is some additional information about the drone. How do these factors make the drone an effective tool? What limitations might it have compared with piloted aircraft?

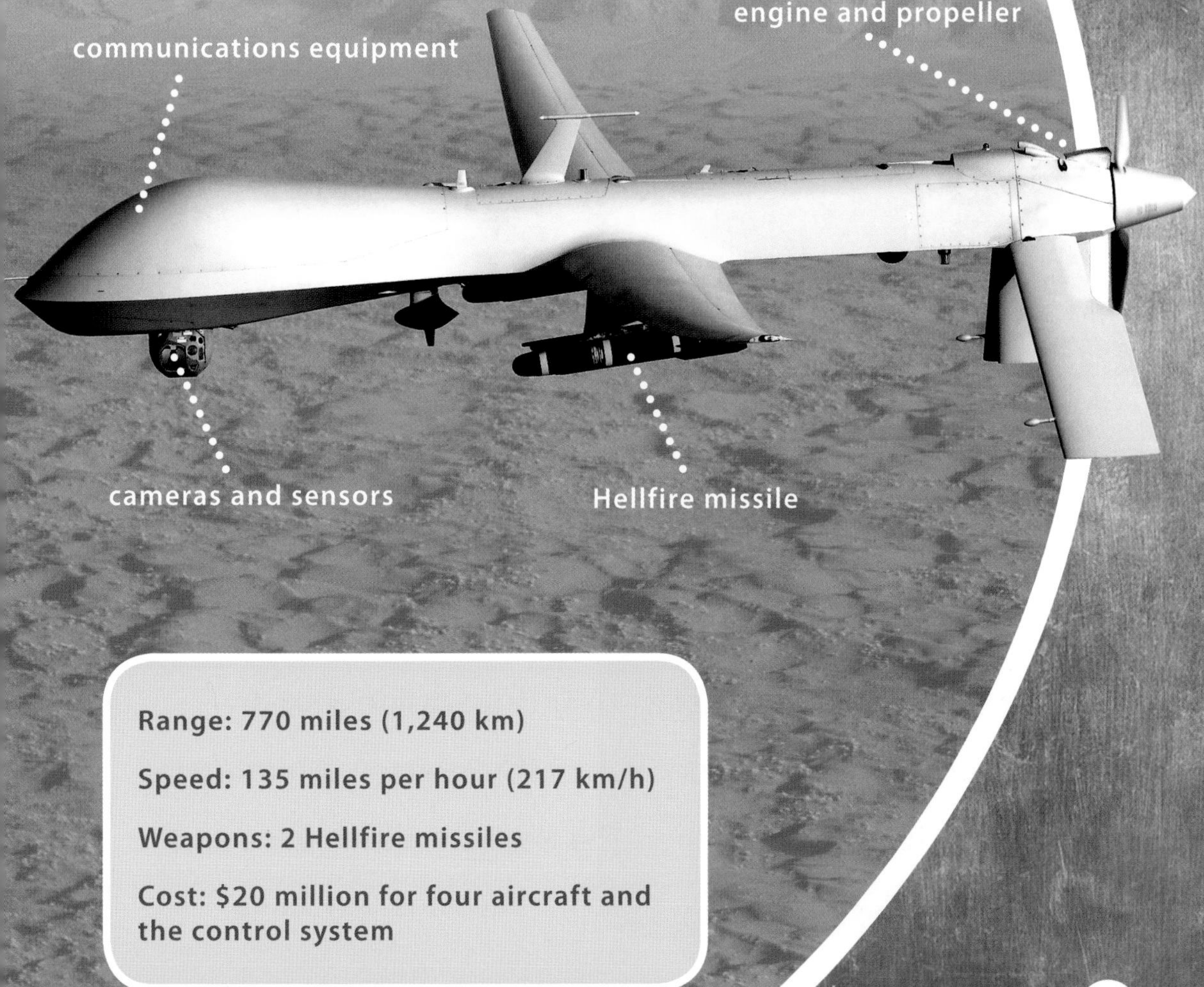

communications equipment

engine and propeller

cameras and sensors

Hellfire missile

Range: 770 miles (1,240 km)

Speed: 135 miles per hour (217 km/h)

Weapons: 2 Hellfire missiles

Cost: $20 million for four aircraft and the control system

Both drones can carry cameras to track enemy movements. This function is called aerial reconnaissance. They can fly quietly above a target for many hours. Two smaller drones also give troops a view from above. The RQ-11 Raven is launched by hand. The larger RQ-7 Shadow is launched from a catapult off the back of a trailer.

The use of drones has been controversial. They sometimes kill civilians by mistake. The military works to be sure that enemy troops are targeted. However, it can make errors. When this happens, innocent people are killed. For drones to be effective, they must be backed up by good intelligence.

GROUND ROBOTS

One of the most effective ground robots is the PackBot. It is a small, flat robot that moves on treads. More than 2,000 PackBots have been used in the wars in Iraq and Afghanistan.

The PackBot has cameras to view its surroundings. It uses an arm to inspect dangerous materials. A special kit lets it dig out buried objects. Sensors in the robot can detect chemicals. The PackBot is powered by batteries. Soldiers operate it with a hand controller.

Another military robot is the Dragon Runner. It weighs only 20 pounds (9 kg). This is light enough to be carried in a backpack. This robot is used to destroy IEDs. It can be thrown over fences or from moving vehicles. The Dragon Runner's camera sends images back to the operator. This allows soldiers to look around corners. The robot uses its arm to place a

Soldiers test a PackBot's ability to climb over rubble.

small explosive charge and blow up IEDs. The soldiers controlling the robot can stand at a safe distance.

STRAIGHT TO THE
SOURCE

On May 23, 2013, President Barack Obama delivered a speech on US drone policy:

> The United States has taken lethal, targeted action against al-Qaeda and its associated forces, including with remotely piloted aircraft commonly referred to as drones. . . . This new technology raises profound questions—about who is targeted, and why; about civilian casualties, and the risk of creating new enemies; about the legality of such strikes under US and international law; about accountability and morality. . . . To begin with, our actions are effective. . . . Moreover, America's actions are legal. . . . We are at war with an organization that right now would kill as many Americans as they could if we did not stop them first. . . . The use of drones is heavily constrained.

> Source: "Obama's Speech on Drone Policy." *New York Times*. New York Times, May 23, 2013. Web. Accessed October 24, 2016.

Back It Up

In his speech, President Obama used evidence to support his main point. Write a paragraph describing the point he makes. Then write down two or three pieces of evidence he uses to support the point.

CHAPTER
FOUR

CYBERWARFARE

A large part of the War on Terror is fought online. Terrorist groups use the Internet to plan attacks. They also use it to recruit new members. The US government works to disrupt these groups' messages. It tries to prevent attacks before they can occur.

TERRORIST GROUPS AND THE INTERNET

There are thousands of active terrorist websites. Some websites teach how to build bombs. Others offer advice on carrying out attacks. Groups may even show videos of their killings.

Some parts of the War on Terror are fought online from ordinary-looking office buildings.

MEETING WITH TECH COMPANIES

On January 8, 2016, government officials met with technology companies. They discussed how technology could be used to help fight ISIS. People from such companies as Apple, Microsoft, and Google were there. One discussion topic listed asked the following: "In what ways can we use technology to help disrupt paths to radicalization to violence, identify recruitment patterns, and provide metrics to help measure our efforts to counter radicalization to violence?"

Government agencies monitor Internet activity believed to be conducted by terrorists. The National Security Agency (NSA) is one of these agencies. In 2009, the NSA intercepted a terrorist e-mail. The man was writing to someone in the United States. He was discussing how to make bombs. The man in the United States was identified. He lived in Denver, Colorado. Police searched his home. They discovered bomb-making materials. The man confessed

The terrorist group ISIS releases video messages to its followers online.

to a terrorist plot. He had planned to bomb the New York City subway system. The police arrested him.

Some terrorist activity on the Internet takes place on social media sites. Terrorists use Twitter, Facebook, and YouTube. They communicate with tweets, posts, and videos. Government agencies are working with technology companies to track and remove such material.

STUXNET

Stuxnet is a computer virus. Most people believe the United States and Israel created it. However, the two nations have not confirmed this. In 2007, experts feared Iran was making a nuclear bomb. The virus reached Iranian facilities. There, it destroyed equipment. Research was set back. Security experts discovered the virus in 2010. Stuxnet was one of the first viruses used against machinery.

WAGING CYBERWARFARE

In 2016, the United States declared cyberwar on the terrorist group ISIS. This group's name stands for Islamic State of Iraq and Syria. The goal of the mission was to disrupt ISIS

Computer skills have become just as important as combat skills for many parts of the military.

activities. The group uses technology to spread its

messages and pay its fighters.

The United States Cyber Command is responsible for US hacking efforts. This branch of the Department of Defense was created in 2010. It wages cyberwarfare. By the fall of 2016, approximately 4,700 people worked there.

Part of its plan is to hack into the terrorists' networks and alter their messages. One goal is to redirect ISIS fighters to areas where US forces can attack them. Disrupting the flow of money online is another goal.

This is not the first time the United States has used cyberwarfare. In 2007, US troops captured enemy computers in Iraq. NSA workers then sent fake e-mails to enemy fighters. They told the fighters to meet at a certain place. There, US troops attacked the enemy. In a few months, more than 4,000 enemy fighters were killed this way.

STRAIGHT TO THE
SOURCE

In April 2015, the US Department of Defense (DoD) issued a report on cyberwarfare:

> *The Defense Department has three primary cyber missions. First, DoD must defend its own networks, systems, and information. . . . The Defense Department must be able to secure its own networks against attack and recover quickly if security measures fail. . . . For its second mission, DoD must be prepared to defend the United States and its interests against cyber attacks of significant consequence. . . . If directed by the President or the Secretary of Defense, the US military may conduct cyber operations to counter an imminent or on-going attack against the US homeland or interests in cyberspace. . . . Third, if directed by the President or the Secretary of Defense, DoD must be able to provide integrated cyber capabilities to support military operations and contingency plans. . . .*

> Source: "The DoD Cyber Strategy." *Defense.gov*. US Department of Defense. April 2015. Web. Accessed January 5, 2017.

Consider Your Audience

How would you adapt this passage for another audience, such as a classmate? Rewrite it for the new audience. How does your new approach differ from the original text, and why?

CHAPTER
FIVE

SECURITY TECHNOLOGY

Identifying terrorists and defending against attacks is an important part of the War on Terror. In the United States, terrorists have bombed buildings, shot people at social gatherings, and more. The best way to stop terrorism is prevent attacks from happening. High-tech tools are giving the police ways to do this.

BIOMETRICS

Biometrics identify a person based on physical traits. These technologies use face recognition, fingerprints, and other methods. Names and

Some elements of security technology, such as those involved in airport security, have become controversial.

documents can be faked. But changing physical traits is much more difficult. In recent years, US officials have studied how biometrics can identify possible terrorist threats.

One alleged planner of the September 11 attacks was captured using biometric technology. In August 2001, Mohammed al-Qahtani was fingerprinted in Florida. He could not explain why he was in the United States. In December 2001, US military forces captured Qahtani on a battlefield. His fingerprints were compared to the ones taken in Florida.

Fingerprint scanning has become a popular biometric technology.

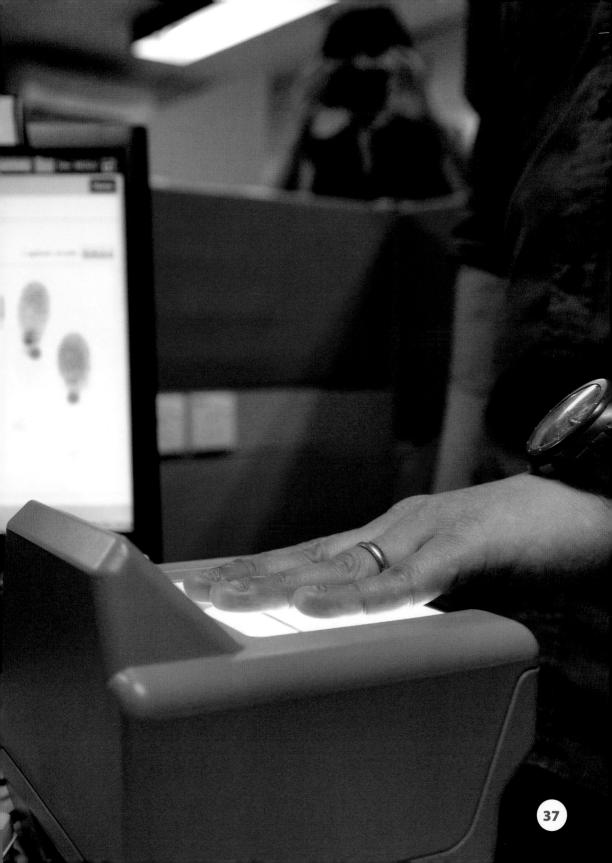

TERRORISM BY THE
NUMBERS

This graph shows the number of deaths in terrorist attacks that targeted Americans in each year between 2001 and 2014. Why do you think that graph has remained relatively flat since 2001? What are the possible reasons this might be the case?

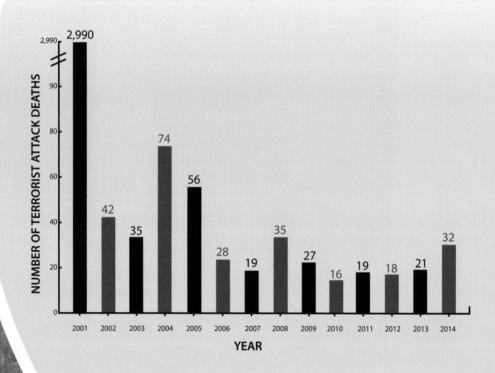

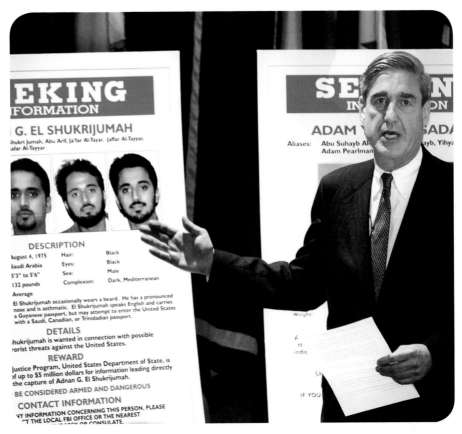

The FBI and other law enforcement agencies sometimes ask for public help in finding terror suspects.

Qahtani was linked to the September 11 attacks. The government charged him with numerous crimes.

The Federal Bureau of Investigation (FBI) operates biometric databases. In 1999, it started the Automated Fingerprint Identification System. The system includes the fingerprint records of 48 million people. The FBI also manages the Next Generation Identification system. This is the world's largest database of biometric information.

Today, the military encourages troops to gather biometric information from prisoners. This data can then be searched for matches.

THE BOSTON MARATHON BOMBINGS

On April 15, 2013, two bombs exploded during the Boston Marathon. Three days later, the FBI released photos of two suspects. The two men were brothers. Shortly after midnight on April 19, police officers killed one of the suspects in a shootout. Later that day, they captured the second suspect. In June 2015, the surviving brother was sentenced to death.

FUTURE TECHNOLOGIES

New devices are being developed to help analyze surveillance photos and video. In 2013, two terrorists set off bombs at the Boston Marathon. They killed three people and injured more than 250 others. In its investigation, the FBI used a tool called BriefCam. It helped them study hours of surveillance footage. It was the key to identifying and capturing the terrorists.

Terrorism is unlikely to go away in the near future. The US government is fighting it on many different fronts. Troops and drones attempt to root out terrorists in foreign countries. Computer experts disrupt terror groups online. And law enforcement works to prevent attacks in the United States. Technological tools help in all these areas. They help save lives around the world.

FURTHER EVIDENCE

Chapter Five mentioned the issue of airport security. The relationship between security and privacy has been highly controversial. Read the article below. Does the article add new evidence to support ideas in the chapter? Does it introduce new ideas about this topic?

AIRPORT SECURITY ADVANCES CLASH WITH PRIVACY ISSUES

abdocorelibrary.com/war-on-terror-tech

IMPORTANT
DATES

2001
Terrorists attack the World Trade Center in New York City and the Pentagon in Washington, DC, on September 11.

2001
In December, the US military uses fingerprints to identify Mohammed al-Qahtani, one of the alleged planners of the September 11 attacks.

2007
The Stuxnet virus attacks Iranian research facilities.

2007
US forces capture enemy computers in Iraq, allowing them to send disruptive e-mails to enemy forces.

2009
The NSA intercepts an e-mail which leads to the arrest of a terrorist planning to bomb the New York City subway system.

2009
Enemy forces in Iraq hack the video feed of a Predator drone.

2011
Navy SEALs kill Osama bin Laden at his compound in Abbottabad, Pakistan, on May 2.

2013
Terrorists set off bombs at the Boston Marathon on May 13.

2013
President Obama delivers a speech on US drone policy on May 23.

2015
In April, the Department of Defense issues a report outlining the nation's use of cyberwarfare in the War on Terror.

2016
On January 8, government intelligence leaders meet with technology companies to discuss how tech tools can be used to disrupt terrorist activities.

STOP AND
THINK

Surprise Me

Chapter Two discusses some of the weapons and tools used in the War on Terror. After reading this book, what facts about these weapons did you find most surprising? Write a few sentences about each fact.

Say What?

Reading about military technology can mean learning new terms. Find five words in the book that you are unfamiliar with. Use a dictionary to find out what they mean. Then write the meanings in your own words, and use each word in a new sentence.

Another View

This book talks about the technology and methods used to fight the War on Terror. Ask an adult to help you find another source about these subjects. Write a short essay comparing and contrasting the content of the new source with the content in this book. How are they similar and why? How are they different and why?

You Are There

Imagine you are meeting with the president of the United States to discuss the War on Terror. What would you ask the president? What advice would you give to the president? Write a letter to your friends discussing your meeting. Be sure to add plenty of detail to your letter.

GLOSSARY

biometrics
technology that identifies a person's physical traits

compound
an area of land, usually fenced in and containing one or more buildings

cyberspace
the online world of computer networks, including the Internet, through which people communicate

databases
sets of related information that are stored in a computer

drones
unmanned aircraft

GPS
the global positioning system, which uses satellites to determine the user's location on Earth

monitor
to regularly check something over a period of time

reconnaissance
military observation of a region in order to gain information

SEALs
members of a special fighting force of the US Navy

stealth
able to move without being detected by the enemy

surveillance
close observation

LEARN MORE

Books

Gagne, Tammy. *Incredible Military Weapons.* Minneapolis, MN: Abdo Publishing, 2015.

Marciniak, Kristin. *Navy SEALs.* Minneapolis, MN: Abdo Publishing, 2013.

O'Keefe, Emily. *September 11 through the Eyes of George W. Bush.* Minneapolis, MN: Abdo Publishing, 2016.

Websites

To learn more about War Technology, visit **abdobooklinks.com**. These links are routinely monitored and updated to provide the most current information available.

Visit **abdocorelibrary.com** for free additional tools for teachers and students.

INDEX

About the Author

Nel Yomtov is a writer of children's nonfiction books and graphic novels. He specializes in writing about history, the military, country studies, and science. Nel lives in the New York City area.